Dedication

Penelope Sunshine Williams a.k.a. Daddy's Penny Pooh, I love you so much sweetheart. You are my world and I love our daddy and daughter bond. I love our ice cream Fridays and I love our monthly slumber parties in your room where we play games and act silly all night. I love our jokes and I especially love our serious talks as well. Remember you can always come to daddy for anything. These memories we share, will always be held close to my heart. I will always cherish them forever. Never stop believing in your dreams and never lose your imagination. And most importantly, never stop loving your crazy, wild, silly, goofy and LOVING Father. Baby, can you believe daddy turned one of our imaginative stories into a book? Penny Pooh with strong faith in God, all things are possible.

Love Always,
Your Daddy-O

I Almost Caught Santa Claus

By: Terry A. Williams

It was Christmas Eve, and they sat next to the tree.
On the couch daddy sat with Penny in his lap,
For her mommy it was a beautiful sight to see.

Daddy gave Penny an excited look.
Then pretended to be Santa Claus,
As he read the last sentence of the book.
"Merry Christmas to all
and to all a good night!
Penny, sweet dreams
and I hope you sleep tight."

Penny said, "Hey! That wasn't a part of the story!"
She went from happy to sad
and she started to worry.
Daddy asked, "What's wrong?
What are you thinking about?"
She then stuck out her bottom lip
and began to pout.

She said, "Daddy I'm not tired,
I don't want to go to bed."
Then a thought came to her mind,
she smiled and said,

"Can we sing Christmas carols?"
As the smile on her face grew.
Daddy answered using her nickname
and said, "How can I say no to my Penny Pooh?
But it can only be one song,
where we both can sing along."
She shouted, "The 12 Days Of Christmas!"
He said, "Whoa! Whoa! That's way too long!"

Penny said sadly,
"Can we sing it still?"
He said, "12 Days Of Christmas it is,
but let's make a deal."

She happily said, "Sure, okay."
He said, "Let's start on your favorite part,
the 5th day."

At the same time they sang:
"♫ On the 5th day of Christmas, my true love gave to me,
5 Golden rings, 4 calling birds, 3 french hens, 2 turtle doves
and a partridge in a pear tree ♫."
In the same melody, daddy added,
"♫ Night, Night PEN-EL-O-PEEEEE! ♫"

Penny asked,
"Can we sing one more song before I sleep tight?"
Daddy said, "Sure, let's sing Silent Night.
Get it? Silent Night."

Then he said in his best Santa voice,
"HO, HO, HO!
Penny you don't have a choice -
to bed you must GO, GO, GO!"
Penny interrupted saying,
"NO, NO, NOOOOOO!"

Penny had that Ooops!
I forgot something look on her face.
She ran into the kitchen like she was in a race,
then came back with milk and cookies
to put by the fireplace.

Daddy gave Penny
a piggyback ride upstairs to her bed.
As soon as she laid down,
she quickly popped up and said,
"What happens if you catch Santa Claus
putting presents under the tree?
What would happen
and what would the outcome be?"

After hearing the question,
Daddy's eyes began to beam.
He was in a daze,
and stuck in his daydream.

Penny tried to interrupt him
and yelled, "Hello daddy are you there?"
Daddy just stood there and smiled,
with an excited stare.

He finally snapped out the daydream,
by shaking his head while quickly blinking.
That's when Penny asked,
"Daddy, what were you just thinking?"

He then said,
"What happens if you catch Santa
is a mystery to us all.
But when I was your age
I almost caught Santa Claus."

Penny's mouth was wide open,
As she said "OMG!
Daddy, Daddy, Daddy this is the story
you have to tell me."

He said, "Okay, okay, okay!"
She screamed, "My daddy almost caught Santa!
NO WAY, NO WAY, NO WAY!"

Daddy sat on the bed,
and began to say,
"I haven't told this story in over 30 years,
but I remember like it was yesterday."

On Christmas Eve,
My brother, sister and I would sleep in the same room.
I was tossing and turning for hours,
then I heard a loud BOOM.

I thought to myself,
"It was probably nothin'.
Just my mom checking on the turkey,
and closing the oven."

Then I heard a quiet footstep.
But I figured it was my Dad,
trying not to wake us while we slept.

I tried to go back to sleep,
by closing my eyes.
Then I opened my eyes wide,
and screamed, "Those footsteps didn't come from the hallway.
They came from outside!"

Then I heard something traveling,
from the top of the chimney on the roof.
And when it hit the bottom
I heard jingle bells with a quiet poof.

I quickly hopped up
and downstairs I zoomed.
When I got to the bottom step,
my mouth dropped when I entered the room.

My heart began to race.
I then looked at Penny,
and she had a shocked look on her face.

When I got downstairs,
I didn't know who I was going to see.
I couldn't believe I saw Santa's shadow
by the Christmas tree.

I tippy toed across the room
to get a better look.
He looked exactly as described
'In The Night Before Christmas' book.

I anxiously hid,
behind the hallway wall.
And said quietly,
"I can't believe I saw Santa Claus."

Santa just finished his last cookie
and with the milk took his last slurp.
He wiped the crumbs off his suit
and let out a little burp.

I came from behind the wall,
because I wanted us to meet.
I took one step on the floor
and the wood made a loud squeak.

I froze.
He froze.
We both stood frozen.
The only thing separating us
was the Christmas tree from the store I had chosen.

I quickly went to the back of the tree,
to give him a hug.
And just that fast,
he was in the front of the tree where I just was.

I went back to the front and he went back to the back.
We both ended up on the opposite side.
"Santa moves fast", I said to myself
as he continued to hide.

Through the branches of the Christmas tree,
I saw his red suit.
There was nothing under the tree,
And I saw the gold buckle on his boot.

I zoomed upstairs to get my bro and sis,
because I needed the proof.
When we came back down,
presents filled the tree and we heard jingle bells leaving the roof.

I stood there filled with joy,
and I gave myself a round of applause.
Then I screamed,
"I almost caught Santa Claus!"

As Santa left the roof
and dashed away all,
he wiped his forehead and said,
"whew, that was a close call."

The End